JOSEPH'S COAT OF MANY COLORS

LA TÚNICA DE MUCHOS COLORES DE JOSÉ

By/ por   Grace Swift

CREDITS/ CRÉDITOS:

Author / Autor: Grace Swift

Illustrator / Illustradore: José Trinidad

Art Contributors / Colaboradores de Arte
8 of my grandchildren/ 8 de mis nietos
Bryan Gregory, Jessica Lynn, Monique Loriann, Jasmine Renay, Alexandria Marie,
Corrie Kashawn, Corben Elshawn and Benjamin Jr."Smoov"

Dedicated to my great-grandchildren /Dedicado a mis bisnietos:
Nekia Richelle, Brianna Gabrielle, Knoah Darwell, Benjamin Jr. III "Trae", Saniah Marie,
Sydney Janea, Stephen Michael Jr. "SJ", Skylee, and Joselyn

Educators/ Educadores: William Gordon Sr., Shelia Trujillo-Trinidad
Translators/:Traductores: Clara Molina, Ana Sherman, Sheila Trujillo- Trinidad,
Antonio Rosa, and David Nolan @ Mississippi State University

Special thanks/ gracias especiales: Mississippi State University Libraries; Nancy
Bardwell. Digital Media Center; Stephanie Agnew, Dorothy Johnson, Rob McDougald
Thomas La Foe, and Digital Media Student assistants: Darion Evans, Dustin Widmer

My home Church, School/Mi iglesia, escuela de origen: Bishop Billy White Sr.,
First Lady Juanita White: Heart to Heart Academy Academia de corazón a
corazón, Administrator Billy White Jr., and Monique White.

Read the true story of Joseph and his coat in Genesis chapter 37
Lea la verdadera historia de José y su tunica en Génesis capítulo 37

Copyright © derechos de autor 2013 by author/ autor: Grace Marie Swift

All material: art and the story line is the work of the author. Any similarities is purely coincidental.
Todo el material: el arte y la historia es obra del autor. Cualquier similitud es puramente coincidente.

None of the text or illustrations can be copied or transferred electronically
without written consent from the author/ publisher.
Nadie de los textos o ilustraciones puede ser copiado o transferido
electrónicamente sin el consentimiento por escrito del autor / editor.

Printed in the United States
Impreso en los Estados Unidos

Translators: Traductores
Ana Stilianou
Clara Molina
Sheila Trujillo
Antonia Rosa

Contributing Art Work
Alexandria Young-Sarver
Benjamin "Smooth" Sarver

Educational Advisors:
William Gordon Sr.
Joan Hunter
Sheila Trujillo

Joseph dreamed one night under the moon and stars

José soñó una noche bajo la luna y las estrellas

One 1 Uno

as his father traveled two cloudy
days.

mientras que su padre viajaba dos
días nublados.

Two 2 Dos

He cut 3 leaves from a tree,

Cortó tres hojas de un árbol,

Three 3 Tres

crossed four waves of the sea,

cruzó cuatró olas del mar,

Four 4 Catro

and climbed five mountains.

y subió cinco montañas.

Five 5 Cinco

He watched his father pick up
six apples,

Veía que su padre recogió
seis manzanas,

Six 6 Seis

seven bananas,

siete guineos,

Seven 7 Siete

and eight grapes.

y ocho uvas.

Eight 8 Ocho

Then his father pulled up nine flowers

Entonces su padre arrancó nueve flores

Nine 9 Nueve

and ten oranges while he
was asleep.

y diez naranjas mientras
dormía.

Ten 10 Diez

His father cut out 11 black rectangles,

Su padre cortó once rectángulos negros,

Eleven 11 Once

twelve white circles,

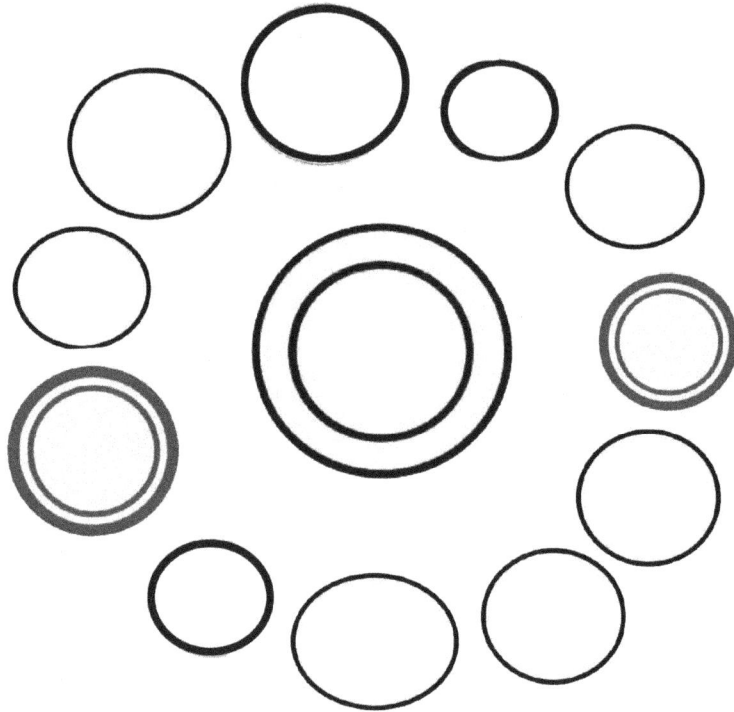

doce círculos blanco

Twelve 12 Doce

and thirteen green triangles.

y trece triángulos verdes.

Thirteen 13 Trece

He stacked up fourteen blocks of blue,

Él amentoné catorce bloques de azules,

Fourteen 14 catorce

added fifteen squares of brown,

añadió quince cuadrados cafés,

Fifteen 15 Quince

sixteen more red apples,

dieciséis más manzanas rojas,

Sixteen 16 Dieciséis

seventeen more yellow bananas

diecisiete más guineos amarillos

Seventeen 17 Diecisiete

and eighteen purple grapes.

y dieciocho uvas moradas.

Eighteen 18 Dieciocho

Joseph's father pulled up nineteen
more pink flowers

El padre de José arrancó diecinueve más
flores rosadas

Nineteen 19 Diecinueva

and twenty slices of orange
while he was still asleep.

y veinte rodajas de naranjas
mientras él todavía dormía.

Twenty 20 Viente

When the sun woke him up he saw the coat with all the beautiful colors.

Cuando el sol lo despertó, vio la túnica con todos los hermosos colores.

It was black like the night

Era negra como la noche

but as white as the clouds
in the sky

pero tan blanca como las nubes
en el cielo

and as green as the leaves
on a tree.

y tan verde como las hojas
de los árboles.

It was blue like the water
of the sea

Era azul como el agua
del mar

and brown like the
high mountains.

y café como las
montañas altas.

The Coat was red like
many apples

La túnica era roja como
muchas manzanas

and as yellow as bananas, too.

y también amarilla como los guineos.

It was as purple as many
grapes.

Era morada como muchas
uvas.

Pink like a flower

Rosa como una flor

and orange just like Joseph's dream.

y anaranjada como el sueño de José.

So everything his father did,

Por eso todos lo que hizo su padre,

32

and everywhere his father went,
the coat, Joseph and God
were always with him,

y todas partes adonde fue su padre,
la Túnica, José y Dios siempre
estaban con él,

because they love each other
with all of their hearts.

porque aman a cada uno con
todo su corazóns.

Color the Puzzle

Coloree el rompecabezas

ENGLISH

a
All
Apples
and / an
as
because
Beautiful
But
clouds
coat
colors
cloudy
climbed
crossed
cut
days
dreamed
down
eight
everywhere
everything
father
flower
full
four
five
flowers
for
from
grapes
got
had
heart
him
high
his
he
it
in

juice
like
leaves
love
made
Many
moon
mountains
More
of
on
out
purple
pink
picked
pulled
red
saw
sky
sea
stacked
square
slices
stars
sun
the
that
then
tree
took
travel
up
under
was
watched
while
water
waves
went
with
woke

SPANISH

añades
Agua
apilan
altas
Amo/aman
arboles
arranco
bajo
blanco
colores
contó
como
cielo
Cruzó
Cuando
Corazón
De/del
despertó
diás
Dormia
el
era
en
Él
entonces
estaban
estrella
fue
flor
flores
guineos
hizo
hojas
hermosos
la/ le
lo
mar

montaña
mienstras
montañas
narado
mas
Muchos
noches
Nubes
luna
nublamos
ocho
olas
padre
para
partes
pero
Porque
que
Rosa
recoger
rectángulos
rebanadas
Rosados
siempre
Su
sueño
sol
soñó
soñaba
todas
tambíen
tan
tenía
túnica
tomó
Tres
uvas
una uno
Un
vio
Y /ya

ENGLISH/ SPANISH

COLORS / COLORES

BLACK /NEGRO
BLUE/ AZUL
BROWN /CAFÉ
GREEN /VERDE
ORANGE/ NARANJA
PINK/ ROSA
PURPLE/ MORADO
RED/ ROJO
WHITE/BLANCA
YELLOW/ ARMARILLO

SHAPES / FORMAS

CIRCLES/ CÍRCULOS
BLOCKS/ BLOQUES
RECTANGLES/ RECTÁNGULOS
SQUARE / CUADRADOS
TRIANGLES/ TRIÁNGULOS
HEART/ CORAZÓN

NUMBERS/ NÚMEROS

ONE / UNO
TWO/ DOS
THREE/ TRES
FOUR/CUATRO
FIVE/CINCO
SIX / SEIS
SEVEN/ SIETE
EIGHT/OCHO
NINE / NUEVE
TEN/DIEZ
ELEVEN/ ONCE
TWELVE/ DOCE
THIRTEEN/ TRECE
FOURTEEN/ CATORCE
FIFTEEN/ QUINCE
SIXTEEN/ DIECISÉIS
SEVENTEEN/ DIECISIETE
EIGHTEEN/ DIECIOCHO
NINETEEN/ DIECINUEVE
TWENTY/ VEINTE

The true story of Joseph's Coat is in Genesis 37
La verdadera historia de la túnica de José en Génesis 37

THE SONSHIP SERIES

BOOKS FOR BILINGUAL LEARNING
ENGLISH AND SPANISH

LIBROS PARA APRENDIZAJE BILINGÜE
INGLÉS Y ESPAÑOL

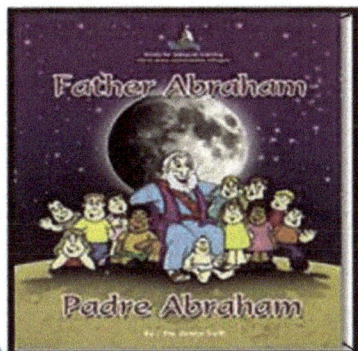

Father Abraham
Padre Abraham
By / Por Grace Swift

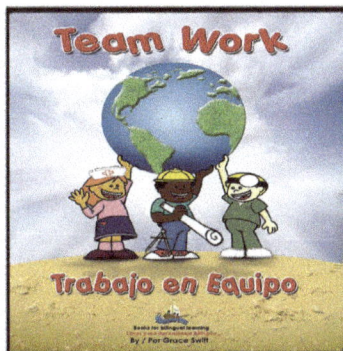

Team Work
Trabajo en Equipo
By / Por Grace Swift

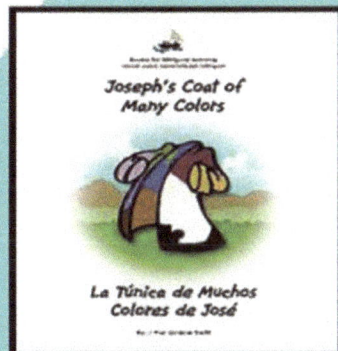

Joseph's Coat of Many Colors
La Túnica de Muchos Colores de José
By / Por Grace Swift

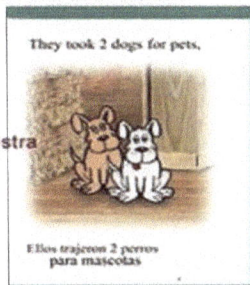

They took 2 dogs for pets,

Ellos trajeron 2 perros para mascotas

sample page
Página de muestra

- Numbers
- Colors
- Animals
- Family members
- Places to go
- Good manners
- Members of the body
- Occupations

- Números
- Colores
- Animales
- Miembros de la familia
- Lugares para ir
- Los miembros de las del cuerpo
- ocupaciones

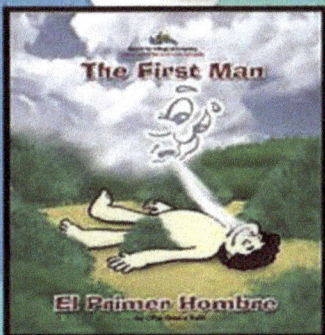

The First Man
El Primer Hombre
By / Por Grace Swift

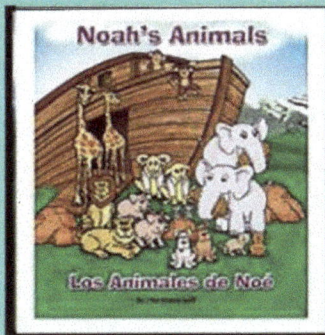

Noah's Animals
Los Animales de Noé

904-460-8855   www.aaadimensions.com/www.sonshipseries.com

www.ingramcontent.com/pod-product-compliance
Lightning Source LLC
Chambersburg PA
CBHW040254100426
42811CB00011B/1255